Contents

Any words appearing in the text in bold, **like this**, are explained in the glossary.

Why do we need to eat?

Most people eat two or three main meals a day. We eat because we get hungry and because we enjoy the taste of food. At the same time we fulfil one of the body's **essential** needs – we supply it with the **nutrients** it needs to stay alive and healthy.

Cells

Your body is made up of millions of tiny **cells**. For example, your bones consist of bone cells, and your skin of skin cells. Most cells are so small you need a microscope to see them, but each one is like a miniature factory, working hard to carry out a particular task. To do this, your cells need a constant supply of **energy**. They also need many different chemicals, which come mainly from your food. These chemicals are called nutrients.

This family is eating a meal that contains several different types of food – rice, meat, vegetables, bread, and milk. Each of these foods contains a mixture of nutrients.

Proteins

for a Healthy Body

Angela Royston

www.heinemann.co.uk/library
Visit our website to find out more information about **Heinemann Library** books.

To order:
☎ Phone 44 (0) 1865 888066
🖹 Send a fax to 44 (0) 1865 314091
🖥 Visit the Heinemann Bookshop at www.heinemann.co.uk/library to browse our catalogue and order online.

Edited by Louise Galpine, Catherine Clarke, and Claire Throp
Designed by Victoria Bevan and AMR Design Ltd
Original illustrations © Capstone Global Library Ltd
Illustrations by Geoff Ward and p. 37 BigTop
Picture research by Mica Brancic
Originated by Steve Walker
Printed and bound in China by CTPS

ISBN 978 0 431 16727 5 (hardback)
13 12 11 10 09
10 9 8 7 6 5 4 3 2 1

ISBN 978 0 431 16733 6 (paperback)
13 12 11 10 09
10 9 8 7 6 5 4 3 2 1

British Library Cataloguing in Publication Data
Royston, Angela
Protein. – 2nd edition – (Body needs)
613.2'82
A full catalogue record for this book is available from the British Library.

Acknowledgements
We would like to thank the following for permission to reproduce photographs: ©Alamy: p. **8** (Self/Pierre Bourrier); ©Corbis: pp. **11**, **27**, **34**; ©FPG: p. **26**; ©Gareth Boden: pp. **4**, **7**, **30**, **39**, **41**; ©Imagebank: p. **23**; ©Liz Eddison: pp. **31**, **38**; ©Photolibrary Group Ltd pp. **10** (Photolibrary RF), **12** (Fresh Food Images/Maximilian Stock Ltd), **40** (Imagestate RM/Foodfolio Foodfolio); ©SPL: pp. **6** (Andrew Syred), **17** (Alred Pasieka), **18**, **21**, **22** (CNRI), **24** (Volker Steger), **28** (Gusto), **29** (BSIP VEM), **33** (Peter Menzel); ©Trevor Clifford: p. **13**.

Cover photograph of eggs in a blue bowl, reproduced with permission of Getty Images/Iconica/Kate Sears.

We would like to thank Dr Sarah Schenker for her invaluable assistance in the preparation of this book.

Every effort has been made to contact copyright holders of any material reproduced in this book. Any omissions will be rectified in subsequent printings if notice is given to the publishers.

Nutrients

Carbohydrates, **fats**, proteins, **vitamins**, and **minerals** are all different types of nutrients. Most foods contain a lot of one type of nutrient but they contain small amounts of other nutrients too. Together, nutrients provide energy and materials that the body needs to work properly and to grow. This book is about protein, what it is, and how the body uses it. However, your body needs other nutrients as well as protein, so we shall first have a look at how these keep you alive and healthy.

Energy food

Your body's main need is for food that provides energy. Everything you do uses energy – not just running and moving around, but thinking, eating, keeping warm, and even sleeping. Carbohydrates and fats provide energy. The body uses carbohydrates just like a car engine burns petrol, and it needs a big supply every day. Foods such as bread, pasta, potatoes, and sugar are mainly made of carbohydrates and are your body's main source of energy.

Fats

Fats provide even more energy than carbohydrates. Foods that include butter, **oil**, or margarine contain fats, and a small amount of them can supply a lot of energy. However, if you eat more carbohydrates or fats than your body needs for energy, it stores the extra as body fat. Some body fat is useful because it helps to keep you warm, but too much body fat can become unhealthy.

OTHER ESSENTIALS

Apart from nutrients, your body relies on food for two other essential ingredients: water and **fibre**. You need to drink at least 6–8 glasses a day to make up for the liquid you lose. Fibre is the undigested parts of food that helps to keep your digestive system working well.

Importance of protein

Protein is important because you need it to make new cells. Each cell consists mainly of water and protein. Your body has to repair and replace your cells constantly and, while you are still growing, it has to create millions of extra cells.

Replacing cells

Most of your cells do not live as long as you do. Skin cells, for example, each last only about 25 days. Your body is making huge numbers of cells all the time to replace those that have worn out and broken down. For example, it makes about 2,300,000 new red blood cells every single second. Red blood cells are manufactured in the **bone marrow** at the centre of some bones and released into the blood. Most types of cells, however, are made in the place where they are needed. Skin cells are made in the lower layers of the skin and stomach cells are made in the wall of the stomach.

Through a microscope you can see the dead cells on the surface of your skin. As dead cells flake off, new cells are produced to take their place.

Growing

From the time you are born until you are an adult, your body is continually growing. It grows so slowly that you do not normally notice the change. Even so, while you are a child, your body is having to make millions of extra new cells to produce bigger bones, extra blood and skin, and so on. This means that it is particularly important for children to eat foods that contain a lot of protein.

Protein in food

Meat, fish, eggs, milk, cheese, and beans all contain a lot of protein. Your body cannot use the proteins in the form that you eat them. First it has to break them down into separate units called **amino acids**. Then your body rebuilds the units into the particular proteins that it needs. If your food does not give you enough energy, your body can use the units of protein to make energy instead.

Vitamins and minerals

Your body needs small amounts of some vitamins and minerals to help it build new cells. For example, calcium is a mineral that makes your bones strong. Cells also need particular vitamins and minerals to work properly. This means that as long as you eat many different types of food, you will get all the vitamins and minerals you need.

Body fact

You cannot see new body cells appearing, but they are doing it all the time. Cells are so small, that it would take about 100 of them laid end to end to measure just 1 millimetre!

Many people grow fast between the ages of 10 and 15. This boy has grown out of his pyjamas!

What is protein?

Protein is one of the essential components of living cells. There are thousands of different types of protein in the human body, in plants and in animals. Proteins in food provide the raw materials from which all the cells in our bodies are built.

Protein in the body

Much of your body is made of different types of protein. Muscles, for example, consist mostly of one type of protein, while bones contain another type of protein. Hair, nails, and the outer layer of skin do not look alike but they are all made of **keratin**. This is a protein that makes them hard and tough. Skin does not feel hard, but it is covered with tough flakes of keratin that make it waterproof. Animals use keratin, too. It is the substance that forms feathers, horns, claws, and scales.

Types of protein

Your body makes thousands of different proteins from a small number of simple chemicals. It can do this because the simple chemicals are put together in a very complicated way.

Proteins are made up of combinations of smaller units called amino acids. Each amino acid is made up of a particular combination of a few simple chemicals.

« Hair and nails are both made of the protein keratin. Nails are hard and brittle, but hair is softened by natural oil, which makes it sleek and bendy.

Amino acids

Amino acids all contain the chemicals **carbon**, **hydrogen**, **nitrogen**, and **oxygen**. Most also contain **sulphur** and some include **phosphorus**. Different amounts of these chemicals combine together in different ways to make various amino acids. Amino acids are the building blocks of proteins.

PROTEIN FACT

Most molecules of protein contain around 500 different amino acids, although some have more and others have less.

Chains of amino acids

A protein is made of several different amino acids linked together, rather like beads in a necklace, to form a chain. Each type of protein consists of a different **sequence** of amino acids. Plants and animals only use about 20 different types of amino acids to form these chains, but they can be arranged in so many different ways that they form thousands of different proteins. The beads in a necklace are linked together by a thread, but in a **molecule** of protein, the amino acids are held together by **chemical bonds** called **peptide bonds**.

A protein is a linked chain of amino acids. A simple chain or strand is called a **peptide**. A peptide may be straight or bent into a three-dimensional shape. A complete protein molecule contains one or more peptide chains.

amino acid

peptide

part of protein molecule

Protein from food

All the different proteins in our bodies are made from just 20 different amino acids. The body can make eleven of these amino acids itself, but the remaining nine must come from our food. These nine amino acids are called essential amino acids because we cannot do without them. Some types of food contain much more protein than other types, and some foods contain all the amino acids we need.

Passing on protein

Plants make all of their own proteins from the nutrients they take in from the soil and from water. When cattle, sheep, and other animals feed on plants, their bodies change the plant proteins into animal proteins. This means that food from plants and from animals both contain protein. The muscles of animals, however, are particularly rich in essential amino acids. Meat from animals contains all of the nine amino acids our bodies need to be healthy, so animal foods are said to be a complete source of protein for humans.

These foods are all rich in animal protein. They contain all the amino acids that humans need.

Meat

Most of the meat we eat comes from different animals' muscles. When you eat chicken breasts, for example, you are eating the large muscles the bird used to flap its wings. Beef, lamb, and pork are mostly the muscles of cattle, sheep, and pigs. We cook them and eat them as steak, chops, mince, and roast meat. Other parts of animals contain protein, too. Some people eat liver or kidneys, for example. Sausages contain mince, but it is mixed with the ground-up liver, heart, and other parts of the animal.

Seafood

Seafood includes fish and shellfish. White fish contains less fat than **red meat**, and is a healthy source of protein. The white or coloured flesh of fish, such as cod, haddock, tuna, salmon, and sardines, are the muscles that lie along each side of the fish's backbones. When you eat prawns, shrimps, lobster, and other shellfish, you are eating their muscles, too.

Eggs and milk

Eggs and milk are also a good source of animal protein. Egg white is mainly protein, while the yolk is a mixture of fat, protein, minerals, and vitamins. The milk we drink comes mainly from cows, but cows' milk is also made into cheese, yoghurt, and butter. Some yoghurt and cheese is made from sheeps' or goats' milk.

Cows spend much of the day and night eating grass. Their bodies turn the proteins in grass into animal proteins of different types. They pass those proteins on to us in the form of milk and meat.

Vegetable protein

Although plant protein is called vegetable protein, it comes mainly from plants that we do not think of as vegetables – nuts, cereals, and **pulses**. Nuts not only contain protein, but also many vitamins, minerals, and oils.

Cereals

Cereals are usually eaten as a source of carbohydrates, but they contain vegetable protein, too. Cereals include wheat, rice, maize, and oats. Wheat is ground into flour and made into bread, cakes, and pasta. Breakfast cereals are also a good source of vegetable protein.

Beans, peas, and lentils

Beans, peas, and lentils are called pulses and they contain plenty of vegetable protein. The Mediterranean dip houmous is made from chickpeas. Some Indian foods, such as dahl, are made from lentils. Beans include broad beans, kidney beans, and haricot beans, which are used to make baked beans. Soya beans are a particularly important source of protein.

Pulses are rich in protein. For most people, about one-third of the protein in their diet comes directly from plants.

Soya beans

Vegetarians often use soya beans instead of meat. Many of the vegetarian dishes you can buy in the supermarket, such as vegetarian lasagne, are made from soya beans. People in Malaysia, Thailand, and Japan have used soya beans for a long time. They use it to make foods such as miso and tofu, which are full of protein. Many of these dishes are now popular in western countries.

New proteins

You can buy ready-made vegetarian meals in shops. Many of these are made from myco-proteins (a type of **novel protein**). Myco-protein can be grown from **yeast**, other **fungi**, or **bacteria**. The myco-protein is **fermented** and then cooked and flavour is added. It can be flavoured to taste like meat, although most vegetarians prefer to add herbs and spices instead of meat flavours.

A complete meal

Even plants that are rich in protein lack at least one of the nine essential amino acids that we need to get from food. This is not a problem, however, because eating different types of vegetable proteins provides the whole range. Many of the snacks and meals you probably already eat contain a mixture. A jacket potato with baked beans mixes two sources of vegetable proteins. Cheese on toast mixes animal and vegetable proteins, as does breakfast cereal and milk.

PEANUTS

Peanuts are not really nuts. They grow underground and are more like peas than nuts. Weight for weight, peanuts contain more protein than raw steak but lack all of the essential amino acids.

Peanut butter sandwiches are a good source of protein. Both the peanut butter and the bread contain protein, and together they supply all the amino acids you need.

How your body digests protein

Your body cannot use proteins in food in the form that you eat them. This is because they are not the exact proteins that your body needs. They contain the right amino acids, but in the wrong amounts and in the wrong sequences. Food also has to be digested before your body can use the nutrients in it. During digestion the food is broken down into tiny pieces that are small enough to pass through the walls of your gut into your blood. Protein is broken down into peptides and then into separate amino acids.

Chewing

Digestion begins in the mouth, when you crunch and chew your food to break it up. As you chew, **saliva** mixes with the food to form a mushy lump. When the lump is soft enough, you swallow and the food passes down the **oesophagus** into your stomach.

In the stomach

The muscles of the stomach act like a slow-moving blender, churning the food around. The stomach juices are strongly acidic and this, together with the churning, turns the chewed up food into a type of thick soup, called **chyme**. Food usually stays in the stomach for two to four hours, but some food, such as spaghetti and rice, passes through faster. Food that is rich in fats and proteins, however, stays in the stomach for longer.

Stomach juices

The stomach contains a strong acid that attacks the food and kills off germs in it. The acid in the stomach is called gastric juice. It also contains a substance called **pepsin**, which begins to break up the protein molecules into smaller bits (see page 17).

COOKING

Apart from nuts, most of the protein you eat has been cooked. Cooked food is softer and easier to chew than raw food. Cooking also kills germs in meat and fish and so makes it safer to eat.

In the intestines

The chyme passes slowly from the stomach into the **small intestine**. Juices from the liver and pancreas pour into the small intestine. The intestines make their own digestive juices, too. All these juices work on proteins, carbohydrates, and fats, breaking them into smaller units. The juice from the liver is greenish-brown and is called bile. It breaks up fat into tiny drops.

Breaking down proteins

Chemicals in the juice from the pancreas work on the protein molecules, breaking them down into shorter and shorter strands. Eventually the shorter strands are broken into separate amino acids.

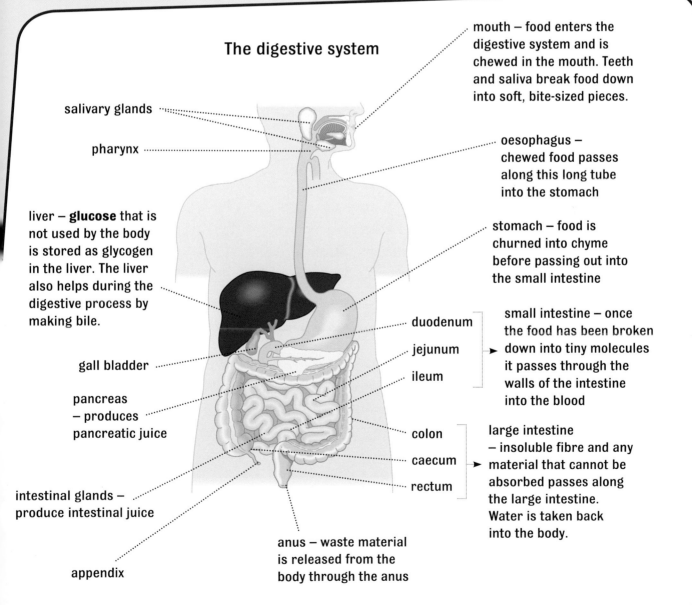

The digestive system

mouth – food enters the digestive system and is chewed in the mouth. Teeth and saliva break food down into soft, bite-sized pieces.

salivary glands

pharynx

oesophagus – chewed food passes along this long tube into the stomach

liver – **glucose** that is not used by the body is stored as glycogen in the liver. The liver also helps during the digestive process by making bile.

stomach – food is churned into chyme before passing out into the small intestine

duodenum

jejunum

ileum

small intestine – once the food has been broken down into tiny molecules it passes through the walls of the intestine into the blood

gall bladder

pancreas – produces pancreatic juice

colon

caecum

rectum

large intestine – insoluble fibre and any material that cannot be absorbed passes along the large intestine. Water is taken back into the body.

intestinal glands – produce intestinal juice

anus – waste material is released from the body through the anus

appendix

Enzymes

Enzymes are the special ingredients in digestive juices that break up large molecules into smaller pieces. An enzyme is something that enables a **chemical change** to take place, without being changed itself. In digestion, different types of food require one or more different enzymes.

How enzymes work

An enzyme attaches itself like a key in a lock to a particular type of molecule. In digestion, this makes the molecule split in two. This is the chemical change. The enzyme then separates and attaches itself to another similar molecule. Enzymes work very fast – a single enzyme can split a million different molecules one after the other in just one minute.

The right conditions

Digestive enzymes only work in the right conditions. The temperature, for example, must be less than 40° C (104° F). The temperature of the body is usually around 37° C (98.6° F) – just right for enzymes. Outside the body, food needs to be heated to around 100° C (212° F), before it begins to break down. Enzymes allow us to digest food at a much lower temperature.

The enzyme trypsin, which helps to digest protein, is shown magnified here. It is one of the two enzymes in the digestive juices made by the pancreas.

Digestive juices

An adult produces about 10 litres (17.8 pints) of digestive juices every day. Of this, 1.2 litres (2.1 pints) is saliva and 3 litres (5.3 pints) is gastric juice.

Pepsin

When you start to chew, your mouth produces extra saliva. At the same time, your stomach produces gastric juices. These juices contain the enzyme called pepsin, mixed with **hydrochloric acid**. Pepsin starts to work on the huge molecules of protein, breaking them into shorter strands of amino acids.

Enzymes from the pancreas

The digestive juice produced by the pancreas contains several enzymes, two of which work on proteins in the small intestine. They break protein molecules into shorter and shorter strands. They do this by cutting the peptide bonds that hold the amino acids together in the chain. These short strands are finally broken into single amino acids.

Babies

When a baby is born, its digestive system has to start working for the first time. It is fed on milk, either from its mother or from a bottle. Babies' stomachs produce an extra enzyme, called rennin. It changes the protein in milk into a solid called casein. This solid takes longer to pass through the intestines, and so gives the other enzymes longer to work on breaking it down.

In the stomach some of the long chains of amino acids are cut into shorter strands. The process continues in the small intestine where the shorter strands are broken into single amino acids.

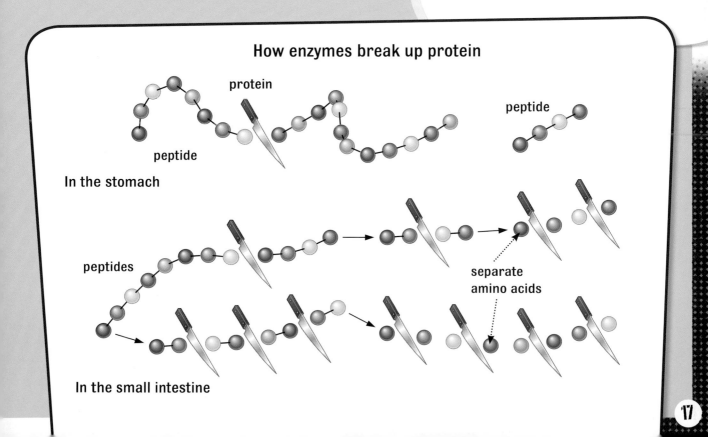

How enzymes break up protein

protein

peptide

peptide

In the stomach

peptides

separate amino acids

In the small intestine

Absorbing stuff

Once the molecules of protein have been broken down into separate amino acids, they pass right through the walls of the small intestine into the blood. The blood takes all the particles of digested food straight to the liver. The liver is an amazing organ that controls hundreds of different **chemical reactions**. One of the liver's many functions is to monitor the level of nutrients in the blood, releasing fresh supplies as they are needed.

Through the intestine walls

The surface of the small intestine is lined with millions of tiny bumps, called **villi**. Each villus is only about 0.5 millimetres long and there are up to 40 villi in each square millimetre. These tiny bumps give a much larger surface for digested food to pass into the blood. Their walls are so thin that digested food passes through them into the blood vessels inside.

The liver

A vein takes the blood, with amino acids and other particles of digested food, straight from the intestine to the liver. The liver uses some of these nutrients to restock the blood. Your liver can store some excess nutrients, such as sugar, but it cannot store excess amino acids.

This magnified photo shows some of the tiny finger-like projections called villi in the small intestine. Nutrients pass through the walls of the villi into the blood.

Instead it changes some of them into sugar and some into other amino acids. The liver then changes any leftover amino acids into a waste substance called **urea**. Urea dissolves in water to form urine and leaves your body through the bladder.

How nutrients reach your cells

Blood, freshly stocked with nutrients, leaves the liver and returns to the heart. The heart sends it to the lungs to pick up oxygen and then pumps it through your **arteries** to all the cells in your body.

Undigested food

Not all protein in your food is digested. Some of it gets to the end of the small intestine before it has been broken down into small enough strands to pass into the walls of the gut. Instead these larger strands pass into the large intestine with other undigested food and slowly make their way to the rectum, from where they leave the body as solid waste.

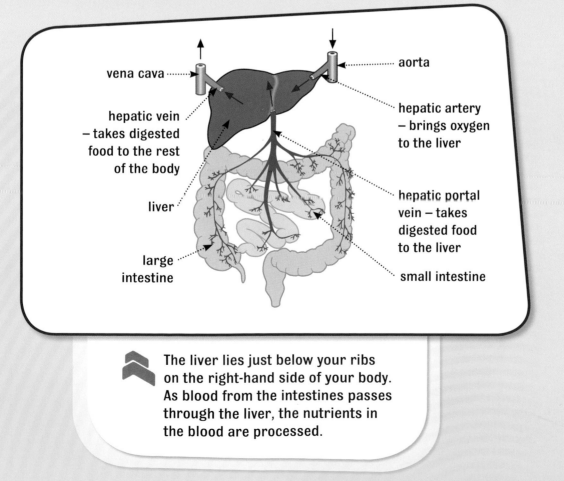

vena cava

hepatic vein – takes digested food to the rest of the body

liver

large intestine

aorta

hepatic artery – brings oxygen to the liver

hepatic portal vein – takes digested food to the liver

small intestine

The liver lies just below your ribs on the right-hand side of your body. As blood from the intestines passes through the liver, the nutrients in the blood are processed.

Using protein

The cells in the body use protein in several different ways. Each cell takes the amino acids it needs from the blood and uses them to build up new proteins. The cell then uses these new proteins to build new cells or to help it carry out its function.

Protein in the cells

Each cell is made up of several specialized parts. Some parts of the cell are particularly concerned with protein. Every cell has **ribosomes** and a Golgi complex. Ribosomes are microscopic factories that make proteins. To do this, they join together the right amino acids in the right order. Different types of cells make different proteins in their ribosomes. The proteins are then stored in the Golgi complex. This strange-shaped structure is a type of warehouse, where the proteins are kept until they are needed. A thin covering, called the cell membrane, surrounds the cell. This membrane is made of protein and fat.

Each cell is like a factory with several specialized units. One type of unit makes protein, which is stored in a different type of unit.

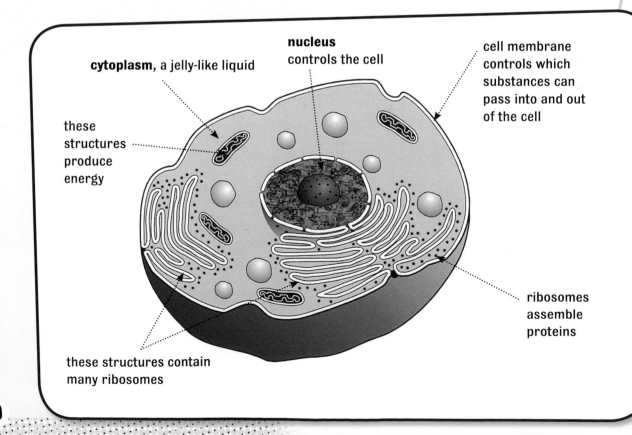

cytoplasm, a jelly-like liquid

nucleus
controls the cell

cell membrane
controls which
substances can
pass into and out
of the cell

these
structures
produce
energy

ribosomes
assemble
proteins

these structures contain
many ribosomes

Haemoglobin

Protein plays an essential role in helping your body function properly. Red blood cells, for example, contain the protein haemoglobin. In the lungs, the haemoglobin in red blood cells picks up oxygen gas from the air you have breathed in. The oxygen turns the haemoglobin bright red. This bright red blood is pumped by the heart through the arteries to different parts of the body. The arteries branch into thinner and thinner tubes called capillaries. The thinnest tubes are so narrow the red blood cells have to change shape to squeeze through them. Here, oxygen moves from the haemoglobin through the wall of the capillary and into the cells that need it. As the blood loses its oxygen, it becomes a darker red. Dark red blood returns through the veins to the heart and lungs, where it collects a fresh supply of oxygen.

Collagen

Many parts of your body contain the protein collagen, which is both very strong but also very flexible, or bendy. Collagen fills the spaces between the cells in bones, ligaments, tendons, and other tissues in the body. Ligaments are stretchy bands that hold a joint together, but allow it to move. Tendons are similar bands of tissue that attach the muscles to the bones. Collagen is also found in the skin and in the walls of blood vessels. Blood vessels have to be very strong and able to stretch as the heart pumps spurts of blood through them.

Collagen protein provides the structure for your bones, ligaments, tendons, and many other parts of your body.

Proteins on the move

Proteins made in some types of cells are released from the cells to do their work elsewhere. Some proteins, such as **antibodies** and **hormones**, are carried by the blood to other parts of the body.

Antibodies

Antibodies are proteins that are part of the body's defence against infection. They are made by cells in the bone marrow, the red jelly-like substance at the centre of some bones. Each type of antibody is specially designed to attack a particular type of bacteria, **virus**, or poison. Some antibodies attack viruses. They latch on to a virus and make it easier for other blood cells to kill it. Other antibodies deal with bacteria. Even when the infection is over, some of the antibodies remain in the blood. This means that, if the same virus or bacteria invades the body again, the antibody is ready to attack it immediately.

 This is what an antibody looks like under a microscope.

Hormones

Hormones are proteins that work as chemical messengers. They trigger various processes in the body. Each type of hormone is made in a particular gland. For example, the hormone adrenaline is made by two glands just above the kidneys. When you are frightened or alarmed, the glands produce extra adrenaline. Adrenaline prepares the body for action – it makes your heart pump faster and your breathing speed up, and it triggers the liver into releasing more glucose into the blood. Other hormones work much more slowly. For example, growth hormone, produced by a gland in the brain, makes you grow taller.

Producing enzymes

Enzymes are made of protein. Different enzymes are used all over the body to speed up different chemical reactions. Enzymes in the cells help to build up proteins. Other enzymes in the cells help to turn glucose into energy. Some enzymes are used in digestion. The cells of the pancreas, for example, produce two enzymes that break up protein. They are called trypsin and chymotrypsin.

Enzyme fact

Trypsin is one of the enzymes that breaks up protein. It is made in the pancreas, but it is so active it could digest the pancreas itself. To protect itself, the pancreas actually produces a substance called trysinogen. This only becomes trypsin when it reaches the small intestine.

The hormone adrenaline helps athletes perform well. This protein makes them more alert and sends more blood and oxygen to the muscles.

Growing new cells

Amino acids are used to grow new cells, either to create extra ones while you are still growing or to replace existing cells. Most of your cells do not live as long as you do. After a while they die and have to be replaced by new cells. In addition, some cells may need to be replaced because they have been damaged.

Repairing damaged tissue

When you graze or cut yourself, some of your cells are destroyed and blood leaks out of the capillaries through the broken skin. However, blood contains a protein called fibrinogen. When the blood leaks out and meets the air, the fibrinogen changes into a solid called fibrin that forms criss-cross threads over the wound. The threads slow down the flow of blood, until it **clots** and hardens to form a scab. Under the scab, new cells grow to replace the damaged skin cells. Cells inside your body can become damaged, too. Bacteria and viruses, for example, damage cells that then have to be replaced.

Growth

Children and teenagers produce the most new cells. The most dramatic rate of growth took place before you were born, when you grew from a single cell to a baby weighing about 3 kilograms (6.6 pounds) and measuring about 50 centimetres (20 inches) long. In the first two years, babies continue to grow rapidly. By the time they are two years old, they have reached about half their adult height! Growth then slows down but continues, sometimes with faster spurts.

Under a microscope you can see the fibrin cells in a wound. This protein helps to seal the wound while new cells are made to replace the damaged ones.

Puberty

Puberty is the time when your body begins to change from a child's into an adult's. It usually starts around the age of eleven or twelve and lasts until about your mid-teens, but this varies from one person to another and differs in girls and boys. During this time you will shoot up in height. You go on growing more slowly until you reach your full height in your late teens or early twenties. Even then your body still makes extra cells. They fill out your shape, making it sturdier and stronger.

How new cells form

New cells are formed by a process called **mitosis**. The nucleus in a cell makes an exact copy of itself. The cytoplasm inside the cell then divides and forms two cells, each with its own nucleus.

Growth fact

Every human life begins as one cell, produced when a female sex cell is fertilized by a male sex cell. That one cell divides over and over again, forming the different parts of the body. By the time you are an adult that one cell has multiplied into 50 million million cells!

Your body needs to grow new cells as you grow up.

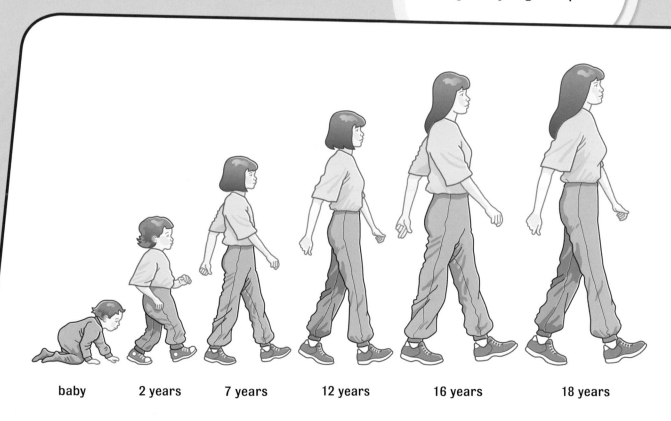

| baby | 2 years | 7 years | 12 years | 16 years | 18 years |

Protein as a source of energy

If the blood contains more amino acids than the cells need, the liver converts some of them into glucose. Glucose is the sugar that provides energy for the cells to function. Glucose contains only carbon, hydrogen, and oxygen, so the cells break down the amino acids, getting rid of the nitrogen, sulphur, and any other chemical not needed for glucose. The glucose may then be released into the blood to supply the cells. Or it may be changed again, this time into a substance called glycogen. This substance can be stored in the liver until it is needed.

Energy first

It is important to eat a good balance of energy-rich carbohydrates and proteins (see pages 36 and 37). If the food you eat does not provide your body with enough energy, then your liver changes amino acids into glucose instead. It does this because the body needs energy more than it needs protein. In some cases, so much protein may be used to supply energy, it leaves the body short of vital amino acids.

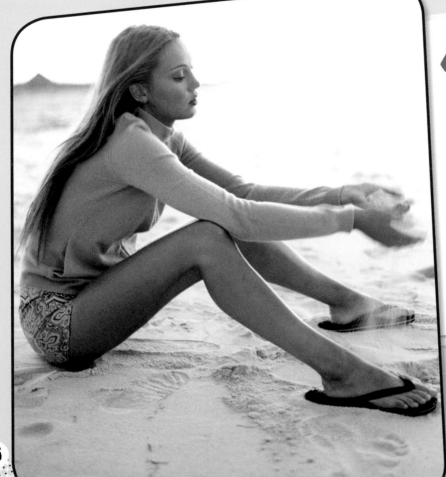

Some people eat very few carbohydrates to keep themselves thin. However, when there is not enough glucose (energy-food) in the blood, the liver changes protein into sugar to provide energy instead. When this happens the body may be deprived of vital proteins.

Athletes and body builders

Athletes may spend several hours every day exercising. The exercise strengthens their muscles and makes their heart and lungs grow larger and work better. Some sports demand a lot of strength or endurance, that is, the ability to keep going. Weightlifting, for example, demands strength, while running a marathon demands endurance. Athletes who take part in these sports often eat a lot of extra protein in their diets, but their diets probably include more than enough protein already. If the extra protein is not needed to build muscle, it will be broken down and used to supply energy instead.

Waste protein

The body can store extra carbohydrates and fats to use when it needs them, but it cannot store protein. If you eat more protein than your body needs, the liver will change some of the amino acids into glucose or glycogen, but the rest is lost as waste.

As she exercises, this woman's muscles use some extra protein to become thicker and stronger. Weightlifting develops muscles.

Too much protein

All the cells in the body need protein so they can keep healthy. It is also needed to make new cells. But is it possible to eat too much of this essential body-building substance? The answer is yes! When you consume more energy than you use up, the body stores the excess energy as fat. So too much food, including too much protein, will make you overweight.

The body stores excess carbohydrates, fats, and protein as fat, so eating too much fast food will make you overweight.

Protein waste

The liver processes protein to release the amino acids the body needs. If there is an excess of protein it changes some into glucose. Then the liver changes any remaining amino acids into a waste substance called urea. The process of changing amino acids into glucose produces waste nitrogen. This is also changed into urea. As the cells use amino acids they also produce nitrogen as a waste product, and it is taken in the blood to the liver and changed into urea as well.

The kidneys

The kidneys are two organs, one on each side of the spine, just above your waist. As blood passes through them, the kidneys filter the blood and remove urea and any excess water and salt. Urea is a solid, but it dissolves easily in water to form urine. Urine trickles from the kidneys down two tubes to the bladder. Urine is stored in the bladder, which gradually stretches as it fills up. It can hold up to about 600 millilitres of urine at a time. When you urinate, you empty your bladder.

Excess protein

People who take in too much protein over a long time may damage their liver and kidneys. Eating too much protein causes problems because calcium in the bones is pulled out to help dilute (weaken) the acid properties of protein. This results in the bones becoming weaker. Eating more protein than is needed can also cause dehydration.

The liver has to work hard to change all this excess protein into urea. The kidneys have to work hard to filter it from the blood.

The kidneys process about two pints of blood every minute. The urea and water is filtered out to make urine, which is stored in the bladder before urination.

UREA

Nitrogen is an important nutrient that plants need to grow. Urea is rich in nitrogen. It is manufactured artificially and used as a **fertilizer** in gardens and on crops. Urine, however, does not make a good fertilizer since it is too acidic. Artificial urea is also used in cattle feed, plastic, and in medicines.

Food allergies

A small number of people react to a particular protein in their food. These are people who are allergic to certain substances, such as the protein in cows' milk, wheat, or nuts. Some people are not allergic to wheat, but their body cannot digest it.

Allergies to protein

When a person is allergic to a particular type of food, their bodies react as though that food were a germ or a poison. Peanuts, milk, cheese, eggs, and wheat are the most common causes of food allergy. The most common symptoms of a food allergy are vomiting and an itchy skin rash. Some people may also have difficulty breathing. The best way to treat an allergy is to avoid the food that triggers it, but this is easier said than done. People who are allergic to peanuts, for example, cannot eat anything until they have checked the list of ingredients on the label. It is difficult because some foods do not contain peanuts, but might have been cooked in peanut oil. They also need to make sure the food has not touched anything with peanuts in it, for example, in a bakery.

If you are allergic to milk you need to read the ingredients listed on food labels to see if they contain milk.

SHARON'S STORY

Sharon is allergic to nuts. When she eats anything that contains even just a small amount of nuts, her body immediately reacts. Within a few minutes, her mouth swells up and she begins to vomit. Her skin breaks out in a red, blotchy rash, which is very itchy. These symptoms can last for several hours. Sharon tries very hard to avoid eating nuts!

Gluten

Gluten is a mixture of two proteins and is the substance that makes bread dough stretchy and bouncy. Bread companies sometimes add extra gluten to the dough to make it softer and lighter. Some people's digestive systems cannot cope with gluten. In many cases this is not because they are allergic to gluten, but because the gluten damages the villi on the small intestine. The gluten wears away the villi so that other nutrients may not be absorbed either.

Coeliacs

People who cannot tolerate gluten are said to suffer from coeliac disease. They have to avoid any foods that contain gluten. Wheat has more gluten than other cereals, but rye, oats, and barley contain some, too. The only common cereals that are gluten free are rice and corn.

EXTREME SHOCK

Some people are so allergic to a particular food their bodies go into extreme shock, also called **anaphylactic shock**. Their blood pressure drops, they become unconscious and, unless they get medical help at once, they will die. Foods that are most likely to cause extreme shock are nuts, shellfish, and eggs.

All of these foods contain wheat. People who suffer from coeliac disease cannot eat any of them.

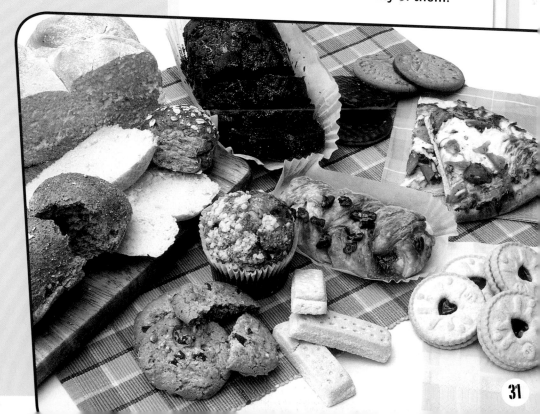

Too little protein

Most people in **developed countries** do not have a problem in getting enough protein. In fact, most people in these countries eat more protein than they need. Only people who have problems with diet, such as those with eating disorders like **anorexia** or **bulimia**, may not get enough protein. Most people who suffer from a lack of protein live in **developing countries**.

Protein deficiency

Many people in developing countries do not have enough money to buy meat, eggs, or other food that contains protein. Children and babies are most affected by not getting enough protein. It affects them in several ways. One of the first signs is that they cannot resist disease very well. Their bodies are also less able to replace worn out or damaged cells, so it takes longer for cuts and wounds to heal. They may feel ill all the time and they cannot learn as well. They do not grow as tall as they should, because their bodies cannot build all the extra cells required for growth.

Kwashiorkor

A severe lack of protein leads to a disease called kwashiorkor. It affects mainly young children who have stopped getting milk (which is full of protein) from their mother and are then fed solid foods that lack protein. In the villages and countryside in much of Africa, the Caribbean, and the Pacific Islands, babies, like everyone else, are fed on yams, cassavas, sweet potatoes, and green bananas — foods that are rich in carbohydrates but low in protein.

Symptoms of kwashiorkor

One of the most obvious signs of kwashiorkor is a large, swollen belly. The swelling can make the baby or child look quite fat. However, it is actually a liquid that has collected below the skin. The liver also becomes larger. The skin becomes flaky and the hair becomes thinner and loses some of its colour. The baby or child stops growing and becomes irritable, tired, and listless.

PEDRO'S STORY

Pedro lives in a remote region of Colombia in South America. His usual diet consists mainly of corn and potatoes, and contains very little protein. He had been ill for two weeks, when his body began to swell. His father strapped four-year-old Pedro to his back and walked for five hours to the nearest medical centre. There, student doctors told him Pedro had kwashiorkor and he was treated in hospital. Two weeks later he was ready to go home, but the students knew that his family still could not feed him properly and that he would probably never grow as well as he should.

This young child is suffering from kwashiorkor, caused by a severe lack of protein in its food. Children with kwashiorkor will die unless they are treated.

Dying of hunger

Famine is the most extreme case of lack of food. People starve when they do not have enough food to supply them with sufficient energy or with proteins. Their bodies become extremely thin and their organs stop working properly. This condition is called marasmus and, unless they find food, they die.

Symptoms of marasmus

People who are starving feel hungry all the time. This is not the sort of hunger that you feel when your stomach rumbles and you are looking forward to a meal. Instead it is a continual pain in the belly and a longing for food. The person loses weight as the body's supplies of fat are used up. Then the body converts the protein in muscle into energy. As their muscles disappear, the shape of their bones becomes clearly visible through their skin. Their ability to fight disease is damaged and they often fall ill. Children stop growing and become tired and irritable. The development of their brains is also affected and they find it difficult to learn or think properly.

How tall you grow does not depend entirely on the amount of protein in your diet. These two children are the same age, but are different heights. Some people grow taller because their parents are tall.

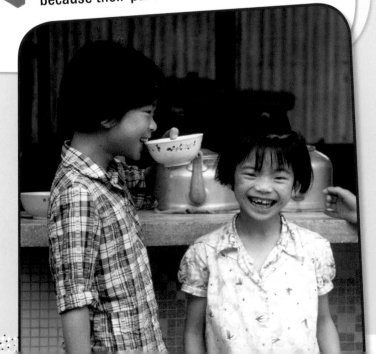

GROWING TALLER

People from poorer countries move to richer countries for many reasons. Their children may eat a different and often healthier diet than their parents did when they were young. When the children grow up they are often noticeably taller than their parents.

Mothers and babies

Pregnant women, mothers, and young children are most at risk in a famine. Pregnant women have to feed both themselves and the baby growing inside them. Once the baby is born, it may feed on its mother's breast milk for up to two years. Mothers need extra protein so that their babies can grow.

Causes of famine

Although the world can produce enough food to feed everyone, millions of people starve to death every year. Most often, people starve because they cannot afford to buy food, particularly food that contains protein.

» TREATING MARASMUS

People who have been starved of food cannot eat large amounts at first. They need to be fed with regular small amounts of water that contains sugar and salts. Gradually they may progress to milk and then to solid food.

These are the parts of the world that are most likely to suffer from famine. They include countries where people are extremely poor and where there is often no rain for months or years.

Area most likely to be affected by famine.

Healthy eating

Your diet is all the food you normally eat. To have a healthy diet, you should eat a variety of food to give you all the nutrients you need – carbohydrates, fats, vitamins and minerals, as well as protein. The eatwell plate divides foods into five food groups and shows the types and proportions of foods that make up a healthy balanced diet.

1 – Bread, rice, potatoes, pasta

This group of foods is rich in carbohydrates. About a third of the food you eat should come from this group. These foods also contain vegetable protein and some important vitamins and minerals.

2 – Fruit and vegetables

Foods in this group are rich in vitamins and minerals. About another third of the food you eat should come from this group. These foods also contain plenty of fibre, which is not a nutrient, but it helps to keep your digestive system working well. We should eat at least five portions of fruit or vegetables every day.

3 – Meat, fish, eggs, beans

Foods in this group include eggs and pulses. Some meats, such as lamb and pork, have more fat in them than, for example, chicken. Adults and children who are overweight should try to choose food that contains protein, but is low in fat.

4 – Milk and dairy foods

This group includes milk, cheese, and yoghurt. These foods are rich in protein but many also contain quite a lot of fat. Young children especially need to eat some fat, but adults and children who are overweight should look for low-fat varieties. Whole milk has the highest fat content. Semi-skimmed milk has most of the fat removed. Skimmed milk has almost no fat, but it is not recommended for children under the age of five years.

5 – Foods full of fat or sugar

This group includes many popular snacks, such as crisps, chocolate, sweets, biscuits, fizzy drinks, chips, and sausages, which are high in fat and sugar. If eaten in excess these foods can make you overweight. You should only eat a small amount of these foods.

RULES FOR HEALTHY EATING

- Eat a wide variety of food.
- Eat most food from groups 1 and 2.
- Eat only a little food from group 5.

The eatwell plate shows the wide variety of food you should eat to enjoy a balanced diet. It is divided into five main groups of food. The space given to each reflects how much of each you should eat.

fruit and vegetables

bread, rice, potatoes, and pasta

meat, fish, eggs, and beans

fatty and sugary foods

milk and dairy foods

Different types of diet

People who live in different parts of the world often eat different foods or prepare food in different ways. Traditional food can be very healthy, because it often uses pulses as well as meat. Many people follow diets for religious reasons that deliberately leave out one or several types of food. Muslims and Jews, for example, do not eat pork, and Hindus do not eat beef. Vegetarians do not include meat in their diets and vegans do not eat anything that comes from animals.

International food

Traditional cooking, from countries such as Mexico, China, India, and Thailand, is often very healthy and is now popular in many other countries, too. Their dishes can use strong spices and particular ingredients, such as water chestnuts, okra, and coconut milk, but most of it is based on familiar food – rice, vegetables, chicken, lamb, and fish. Food cooked in different ways can be tasty and nutritious.

A vegetarian Indian meal can include a wide range of different foods, including rice, lentils, bread, and yoghurt. It provides all the protein you need.

Vegetarians

Vegetarians are people who do not eat meat or fish. They do, however, eat animal protein in the form of eggs and dairy products, such as milk and cheese. This is because eggs and dairy products do not involve killing the animals. A vegetarian diet is perfectly healthy, particularly if each meal includes more than one source of protein. This can be done by mixing pulses, such as soya beans or lentils, with rice or bread, or by mixing animal protein, such as cheese or yoghurt, with vegetable protein. A vegetarian diet is often healthier than a meat-eating diet, because it is likely to contain less animal fats. It is not healthy to eat a lot of these fats.

Vegans

Vegans are people who do not eat any food that comes from animals — they eat only plants. This means that they do not eat milk, cheese, eggs, yoghurt, meat, and fish. Most cakes, biscuits, and other manufactured products contain milk powder or some animal product so vegans avoid them, too. A vegan diet can provide all the proteins that people need so long as they make sure to eat protein from more than one source at each meal. Vegans, however, have to plan their food carefully to make sure they get all the vitamins and minerals they need.

A vegetarian would eat this meal of a jacket potato and cheese, but a vegan would not.

ATHLETES

Athletes, footballers, and other people who play sport do need some extra protein to build up their muscles, but most people eat more protein than they need. Athletes need to include more energy food in their diet, but not more protein.

Healthy snacks

Most people have favourite snacks that they eat when they are hungry between meals. Food companies produce a huge range of snacks that many children like. They include crisps, sweets, chocolate bars, biscuits, and cakes. Most cinemas sell popcorn and fizzy drinks for people to have while they watch the film. Eating too many of these snacks can be unhealthy because they contain a lot of sugar and a lot of fat. However, many other snacks are tasty and healthy. Here are some that are rich in protein without being unhealthy.

Nuts

Nuts are a good snack to eat with your fingers. Peanuts are particularly rich in protein, but many of the packets of peanuts you can buy are too salty. Look for unsalted peanuts and try other nuts, too, such as cashew nuts, walnuts, and pecan nuts. Seeds, such as sesame seeds, sunflower seeds, and pumpkin seeds, all contain lots of protein.

Houmous, taramasalata, and tzatsiki are traditional dips. They are tasty and rich in protein. You can easily make your own tzatsiki by mixing chopped-up cucumber, onion, mint, and garlic into plain or natural yoghurt.

Popcorn

Popcorn is made from corn, which is a good source of protein. The popcorn you buy in the cinema is either very sweet or very salty and costs a lot of money. But it is easy and healthier to make at home, and it is fun too. You buy the raw grain and cook it in a little oil in a pan with a lid. You can hear the corn hitting the lid and sides of the pan as it pops. Don't remove the lid until the grains have stopped popping! While it is still hot, add a little sugar or salt to flavour the popcorn.

ASK BEFORE YOU COOK!

If you are going to make your own snacks, ask an adult first. If you are not used to cooking, you may need an adult to help you. If you use a cooker or hob, make sure you turn it off when you have finished.

A toasted cheese and tuna sandwich is a healthy snack. Sandwich toasters get very hot, so ask an adult to help you if you make a snack like this one.

Nutritional information

The top table shows how much protein you need between the ages of 7 and 14. Based on weight, children need more protein than adults. Pregnant or breast-feeding women need more protein than other adults.

Daily requirement of protein

Age	Protein (grams per day)
All 7–10 years	28.3
Boys 11–14 years	42.1
Girls 11–14 years	41.2

The table below shows amounts of particular foods needed to get your daily requirement of protein. The differences between girls and boys are very small. It is best to obtain your protein from a variety of foods.

Amounts of foods needed to supply daily requirements

Food	7–10 year olds	11–14 year olds
Milk and dairy food		
Whole milk	(900 g) 1.5 pints	(1,300 g) 2 pints
Cheddar cheese	100 g	165 g
Meat and fish		
Roast chicken	a portion (120 g)	1.5 portions (170 g)
Canned tuna	120 g	180 g
Pulses		
Canned baked beans	1.5 medium cans (550 g)	2 medium cans (810 g)
Boiled lentils	380 g	550 g
Cereals		
Wholemeal bread	a third of a loaf (310 g)	half a loaf (460 g)
Cornflakes	12 portions (360 g)	18 portions (540 g)
Snacks		
Peanuts	115 g	175 g
Milk chocolate	340 g	500 g

This table shows how much protein is contained in 100 grams (3 ounces) of a wide variety of foods. It allows you to compare different foods and to work out how much protein is in foods you usually eat.

Average protein content of some foods

Food	Protein (per 100 g)	Food	Protein (per 100 g)
Milk and dairy food		**Meat**	
Milk (full fat)	3.2	Grilled lean, back bacon	25.3
Milk (semi-skimmed)	3.3	Minced beef	23.1
Fruit yoghurt	5.1	Stewing steak	30.9
Cheddar cheese	25.5	Roast lamb	26.1
Boiled egg	12.5	Salami	13.0
		Pork sausages (grilled)	13.3
Cereals		Roast chicken	24.8
White bread	8.4	Roast turkey	28
Wholemeal bread	9.2		
Cornflakes	7.9	**Pulses**	
Cooked spaghetti	3.6	Canned baked beans	5.2
Boiled rice	2.6	Tofu	8.1
		Cooked, dried lentils	7.6
Fish			
Grilled fish fingers	15.1	**Snacks**	
Boiled prawns	22.6	Chocolate biscuits	5.7
Canned sardines	23.7	Peanuts	24.5
Canned tuna	23.5	Houmous	7.6

>> PROTEIN IN PIZZA

A homemade cheese and tomato pizza that weighs 720 grams (25 ounces) contains 61 grams (2 ounces) of protein. If it is shared between four 10-year-old children, it will provide half the protein they need. But if it is shared between four teenage boys, it will provide only about a third or a quarter of their daily requirement of protein.

Glossary

amino acids building blocks of protein. Different amino acids combine together to form a protein.

anaphylactic shock severe form of allergy in which a person's body reacts so strongly to a protein they can die

anorexia eating disorder in which a person eats so little food they become extremely thin and in severe cases may die

antibody cell that attacks a particular type of bacteria, virus, or poison. It is made in the bone marrow and released into the blood.

arteries tubes that carry blood from the heart to different parts of the body

bacteria single, living cells. Most types of bacteria are harmless, but some types can cause disease.

bone marrow jelly-like substance in the centre of some bones. Red and white blood cells are manufactured in the bone marrow.

bulimia eating disorder in which a person often eats a lot of food, but then vomits to rid themselves of it

carbohydrates substances in food that your body uses to provide energy. Foods that contain a lot of carbohydrate include bread, rice, potatoes, and sugar.

carbon one of the most common elements, or simple substances. All living things contain carbon combined with other elements, particularly hydrogen, oxygen, and nitrogen.

cell smallest living unit. The body is made up of many different types of cells, such as bone cells, blood cells, and skin cells.

chemical bond joining together of two molecules due to their chemical structure

chemical change joining of two substances to produce a different substance, or the splitting up of a substance into two or more different substances

chemical reaction *see* chemical change

chyme mushy liquid that passes from the stomach to the small intestine. It is formed from partly digested food mixed with the digestive juices of the stomach.

clot when part of a liquid becomes so thick it forms a soft lump

cytoplasm all the material inside a cell except the nucleus

developed countries wealthy countries that have well established industries and social services, such as transport, education, and hospitals

developing countries poorer countries that do not have well established industries and services, such as transport, schools, welfare

energy ability to do work or to make something happen

enzyme substance that helps a chemical change take place faster without being changed itself

essential so necessary you cannot do without it

famine lack of food that affects most people in a region. Famine leads to starvation.

fats substances in some foods that your body uses to provide energy. Fat is stored by your body in a layer below the skin and helps to keep you warm.

fermented slowly broken down by a fungus, such as yeast, or bacteria to form a new substance

fertilizer chemical or natural substance added to soil to provide nutrients for plant growth

fibre in food, the undigested parts of plants

fungi group of living things that includes mushrooms, yeasts, and moulds

glucose type of sugar

hormones substances produced by different parts of the body that affect or control particular organs, cells, or tissues

hydrochloric acid liquid produced when hydrogen and chlorine combine together. An acid tastes sour or sharp.

hydrogen invisible gas that is one of the gases in air. Hydrogen combines with other substances to form, for example, water, sugar, protein, fat, and hydrochloric acid.

keratin type of protein that your hair, nails, and outer layer of skin are formed of

mineral non-living substance found in the ground. Your body needs certain minerals to function healthily.

mitosis process by which a cell divides to form two new identical cells

molecule smallest part of a substance that can exist and still be that substance

nitrogen invisible gas that is the main gas in the air. Nitrogen combines with other substances to form all the different tissues in your body.

novel protein new type of protein that is produced from fungi or yeast

nucleus part of the cell that controls all the cell's activities

nutrients parts of food that your body needs to get energy, to build and repair cells, and for the cells to function properly. Nutrients include carbohydrates, fats, proteins, vitamins, and minerals.

oesophagus tube through which food travels from the mouth to the stomach

oil in food, a form of fat found in plants

oxygen invisible gas that is one of the gases in air. The body needs oxygen in order to break down sugar to form energy.

pepsin enzyme in the stomach that starts to break down proteins

peptide simple chain of amino acids

peptide bond chemical bond that joins peptides together

phosphorus simple substance that is needed for plants to grow

pulses group of foods that includes lentils, peas, and beans. Pulses are the seeds of some plants and are rich in protein.

red meat meat such as beef and lamb that are usually dark in colour, although pork is also usually described as red meat

ribosomes particles in the cells of the body that build up proteins from amino acids

saliva watery liquid made by glands in your mouth and the inside of your cheeks

sequence several things in a particular order

small intestine part of the intestine into which food passes from the stomach to be digested and then absorbed into the blood. Undigested food passes right through the small intestine into the large intestine.

sulphur simple substance that forms part of most proteins

urea substance formed from waste material in the liver. Urea mixed with water makes urine.

villi tiny bumps in the intestines through which digested food and water is absorbed

virus type of germ that causes certain diseases. Viruses are smaller than bacteria.

vitamins chemicals that your body needs to stay healthy

yeast type of fungus. Yeast is used to make bread and alcohol.